Piece *by* Piece

Machine Appliqué

Sharon Schamber

& Cristy Fincher

American Quilter's Society
P. O. Box 3290 • Paducah, KY 42002-3290
www.AmericanQuilter.com

Located in Paducah, Kentucky, the American Quilter's Society (AQS) is dedicated to promoting the accomplishments of today's quilters. Through its publications and events, AQS strives to honor today's quiltmakers and their work and to inspire future creativity and innovation in quiltmaking.

EDITORS: BARBARA SMITH
         NICOLE CHAMBERS
GRAPHIC DESIGN: ELAINE WILSON
COVER DESIGN: MICHAEL BUCKINGHAM
QUILT PHOTOGRAPHY: CHARLES R. LYNCH
ALL OTHER PHOTOGRAPHY: GENE SCHAMBER

Library of Congress Cataloging-in-Publication Data

Schamber, Sharon.
Piece-by-piece machine appliqué/by Sharon Schamber and Cristy Fincher.
p. cm.
Summary: "Streamlined approach for turned-edge and raw-edge appliqué. Patterns provided for full quilt projects with dozens of designs. Machine appliqué method with how-to-photographs. The pattern for award-winning quilt 'Scarlet Serenade' included"--Provided by publisher.
ISBN 978-1-57432-923-0
1. Machine appliqué--Patterns. 2. Machine quilting. 3. Patchwork quilts.
I. Fincher, Cristy. II. Title.
TT779.S34 2007
746.44'5--dc22

2007011976

Additional copies of this book may be ordered from the American Quilter's Society, PO Box 3290, Paducah, KY 42002-3290; online at www.AmericanQuilter.com. For phone orders only 800-626-5420. For all other inquiries, call 270-898-7903.

Proudly printed and bound in the United States of America

This book
is dedicated to
my daughter,
Cristy. I am so
glad we are
doing a book
together. I also
want to dedicate
this book to my
Aunt Joe. All of
my sewing was
inspired by her.
~ **Sharon**

I dedicate
this book
to my mom
for being my
constant inspiration
and to my husband,
Clay, my son, Aaron,
and, my daughter, Molly,
for loving and supporting
me. I appreciate them
so very much.
~ **Cristy**

Acknowledgments

There are so many people I want to thank for the support they have given me in writing this book:

My husband, Gene, who makes my life easier and keeps me calm. I want to thank him for his endless support and love.

My daughter, Cristy, for being willing to write this book with me.

My sons, Neil and Quinn, for being proud of the progress I have made.

My parents, Leon and Nyetta Larsen. I love them very much.

My students, who really needed an easier method of appliqué. They inspire me to create new techniques that will make quilting easier for them.

The American Quilter's Society staff. I have enjoyed working with all of you.

I would like to thank the many companies that have supported me with products and supplies used in this project:

Bernina® of America for the use of a sewing machine,

Prym-Dritz/Omnigrid® for notions, rotary cutters, rulers and mats,

The Warm and Natural Company for batting, and

Hobbs Bonded Fibers for batting. *Sharon*

There are so many people I want to thank for the support they have given me in writing this book:

My husband, Clay, who makes me laugh and loves me no matter how much time I spend quilting.

My son, Aaron, and my daughter, Molly, for being my true and absolute joys.

My mom for being my inspiration and motivation. She always told me I could sew and quilt, even when I convinced myself that I couldn't.

My two dads, Hal and Gene, for supporting me beyond belief.

The Arizona Quilter's Guild for allowing me the opportunity to teach many wonderful Arizona quilters. *Cristy*

Contents

They say necessity is the mother of invention...

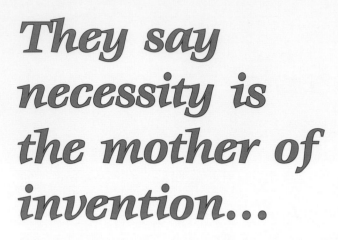

When I started quilting, all I wanted to do was appliqué. I, like many others, tried to do needle-turn, but this technique just didn't work for me. It took way too long to do, and I would lose interest in my projects long before they were done. So I wanted to do my appliqué by machine, but the techniques that were common at the time produced less than appealing results. I was on a path to developing a technique that would work for everyone with ease and efficiency.

The first stop on my path was to use freezer paper with glue to turn the edge. I stitched it down with a hemstitch and then wet the whole thing to pull the paper out. The end result was okay, but it looked like it had been done on the machine, and the process was messy. I wanted a technique that looked more like it was done by hand.

The first foundation was much too flimsy and expensive, so in the next phase of developing the technique, I found the appliqué foundation that I use to this day. It was the answer to my prayers. It took about two years to find the right product. Now, I have it made in bulk for myself and my students. In the process, I have found the right needles and supplies also.

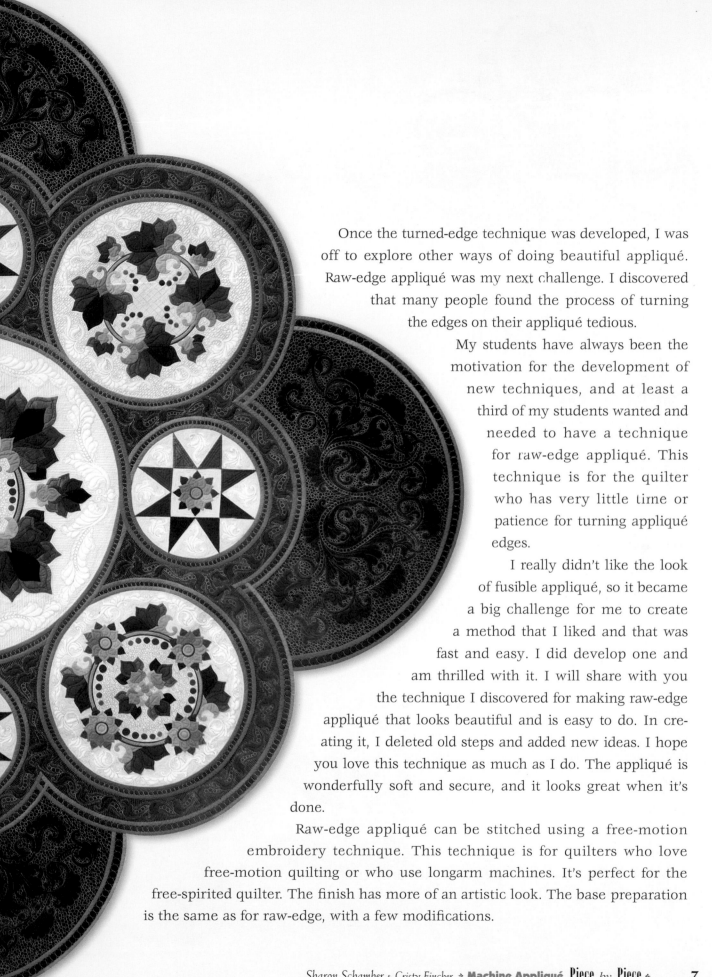

Once the turned-edge technique was developed, I was off to explore other ways of doing beautiful appliqué. Raw-edge appliqué was my next challenge. I discovered that many people found the process of turning the edges on their appliqué tedious.

My students have always been the motivation for the development of new techniques, and at least a third of my students wanted and needed to have a technique for raw-edge appliqué. This technique is for the quilter who has very little time or patience for turning appliqué edges.

I really didn't like the look of fusible appliqué, so it became a big challenge for me to create a method that I liked and that was fast and easy. I did develop one and am thrilled with it. I will share with you the technique I discovered for making raw-edge appliqué that looks beautiful and is easy to do. In creating it, I deleted old steps and added new ideas. I hope you love this technique as much as I do. The appliqué is wonderfully soft and secure, and it looks great when it's done.

Raw-edge appliqué can be stitched using a free-motion embroidery technique. This technique is for quilters who love free-motion quilting or who use longarm machines. It's perfect for the free-spirited quilter. The finish has more of an artistic look. The base preparation is the same as for raw-edge, with a few modifications.

Preparing to Appliqué

Prepare the Fabric

Wash ONLY the appliqué fabric, not the background. Yes, I do see that big question mark that just floated above your head … the reason is … washing the appliqué fabric preshrinks it slightly, so when you wash the whole piece after the appliqué is finished, the folded edges on your appliqué pieces will roll under ever so slightly, hiding the stitches (thus making you look like a genius and master quilter).

Washing the appliqué fabric will also help to eliminate any dye from bleeding into the background fabric. I always wash in hot water and use Synthrapol®. Be sure to follow the directions on the bottle. Wash the fabric as you would normally, but DO NOT dry it in the dryer. This will distort the grain lines and age the fabric. Instead, lay the fabric out flat and let it air dry. Press the fabric flat with a hot iron after it is dry.

Gather Your Supplies

As you may have noticed, some of the items are listed by brand name. While I encourage you to use supplies you already have on-hand, please use the recommended brands, at least to begin with. I have spent much time experimenting with different products and have found some are much more suitable to my techniques than others. After you have mastered these techniques you may want to do your own experimentation.

- Appliqué foundation paper. *This special appliqué foundation paper is revolutionizing turned-edge appliqué. It turns to fiber when it becomes wet so you'll never need to remove it. You can order it from www.sharonschamber.com or www. purpledaisiesllc.com*

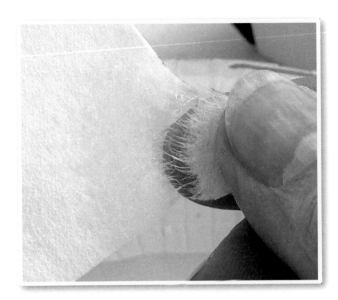

- Cotton embroidery thread. *Use your favorite 50/3 cotton embroidery thread for sewing down the appliqué. Match your thread to the background for turned-edge appliqué. For raw-edge appliqué match your threads to the appliqué.*

- Sulky® Invisible polyester monofilament thread

- Machine embroidery needles 75/11

- Elmer's® Washable School Glue Sticks. *Be sure you don't use a different type of glue stick, even if the brand is Elmer's.*

- Water-soluble basting glue, *with a fine tip*

- Dritz® Liquid Stitch™: Sewing with a Tube

- Spray starch

- 2 manicure cuticle sticks

- Hard pressing surface. *Instructions to make your own are found on page 10.*

- Travel iron. *In my experience Rowenta® and Black & Decker™ travel irons are the only ones that get hot enough, plus they are easy to handle.*

- Freezer paper

- Straight pins

- Stencil brush, *⅜" or ½" work best*

- Large stapler and staple remover

- Fabric and paper scissors

- Sewing machine, *with an adjustable zigzag*

- Washcloth, *to keep hands clean*

Create a Pressing Surface

In my experience as a teacher, I have found that most problems my students have come from the pressing surface they use. It is important to use a surface that is hard and flat. It also needs to have a small amount of grip. To insure successful results for you, I am including instructions for making your own pressing board. My students have found that this board not only helps with the appliqué but also with regular piecing. The board size can be modified to suit your personal needs.

To Make a Small Pressing Board

In my experience teaching, I have found that most problems come from the pressing surface used. It is important to use a surface that is hard and flat. It also needs to have a small amount of grip. Therefore, I am including instructions for making a pressing board. My students have found that this board not only helps with the appliqué but also with regular piecing. The board can be modified to suit your personal needs.

Cut a piece of chipboard that is 22" x 22". Round off the corners.

Spray a small amount of adhesive on the board and place a 22½" square of batting (100 percent cotton) on top.

Fuse a piece of fusible web, 21" x 21", to the batting. Then pull the paper off the web.

Center a 25" square of cotton canvas on the board. Use a hot iron to press it firmly to the batting. The fusible web will secure all the layers together.

Using a staple gun, staple the canvas to the back of the chipboard. Finish the back with a piece of felt, or you can glue a cutting mat to the back.

To Make a Large Pressing Surface

Sometimes I need a larger pressing surface for large blocks and borders, so I have covered my entire cutting table with canvas. The surface is hard enough that if I need to use my cutting mat, I simply place it on top of the canvas and do my cutting. My husband, Gene, also covered my ironing board with the same type of pressing surface.

Iron

I recommend using travel irons, even when not traveling. There are many irons on the market but you want to make sure the iron you use can get VERY hot. The medium to travel-sized irons are also a particularly convenient size to use. Be sure not to use the mini irons — they don't work well at all for these techniques.

1 layer of 100% cotton Canvas

Fusible Web

1 layer of 100% cotton Batting

Chip Board

A New Way to
Turned-edge Appliqué

Before you start to appliqué prewash all of your fabrics as instructed on page 8. Remember to not wash the background fabric.

Trace or print out several copies of your chosen appliqué pattern. You will use these to make your appliqué templates. How many you will need depends on how many appliqué blocks you are making. Generally speaking, you can cut four layers from one pattern.

Trace another copy of your appliqué pattern onto the dull side of freezer paper. This will serve as your master layout pattern when you put your appliqué block together.

Staple the template pattern onto four layers of the special appliqué foundation paper I described on page 9. If you did not get the foundation paper from my website, be sure you are using the type of appliqué foundation paper that does not need to be removed.

With smooth strokes, cut the pieces on the line, through all the layers.

Since we are working on the Tulip Wreath pattern you will want to start with piece 1. Carefully take out the staples.

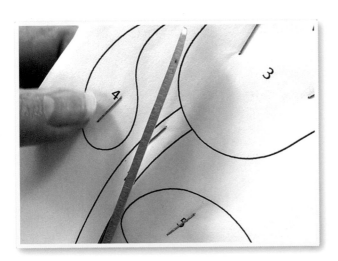

Sharon's Tip: *Be sure to keep all the appliqué template pieces in the same orientation. You may want to lightly mark them just to keep things simple.*

Apply the glue stick (Elmer's Washable School Glue Stick) to the top of the appliqué foundation template and gently place it glue side down on the wrong side of the fabric. Heat-set with a dry iron. This step is essential.

Trim fabric around the appliqué foundation, *leaving about a ⅛" turn-under allowance* beyond the edge of the foundation. The width of a manicure stick is a good measure of the size the allowance should be.

Apply a generous amount of glue stick to the allowance and the edges of the template.

Clip only the **inside** curves of the turn-under allowance, stopping just a few threads beyond the edge of the foundation.

Sharon's Tip: *You'll want to clip after the glue has been applied. If you clip beforehand, the edges will flip up and the allowance will fray.*

Using a pinching action of your thumb and pointer finger, turn the fabric over the edge of the template paper. Use your iron to heat-set the fold. This step is essential. Repeat this process on the other side of your appliqué piece as necessary.

Sharon's Tips & Tricks for …

… when your appliqué has curves:

*Referring to piece 3 in the Tulip Wreath pattern, note that the tulip has both outward curves and inward curves. You will want to CLIP ONLY the INWARD curves stopping a few threads short of the foundation. Remember to apply the glue stick before you clip the seam allowance. **Never clip outward curves.***

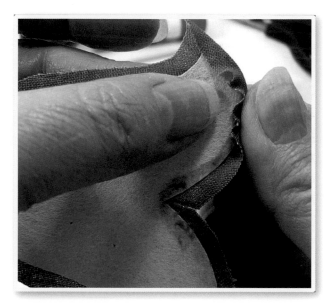

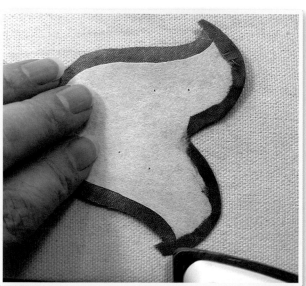

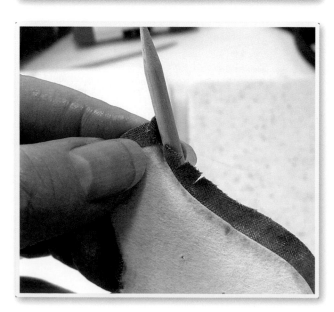

... when your appliqué has V shapes:

Referring to piece 3 again, clip the V in the center of the tulip, leaving a few threads beyond the template. Use the manicure stick, as shown, to turn the allowance at the V. You will find the manicure stick is a wonderful tool to make turns in tight curves as well. Remember to glue first and then clip and turn.

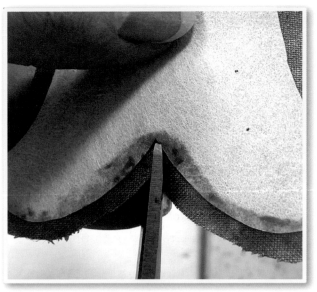

... when your appliqué has overlaps:

Referring to the Tulip Wreath pattern on page 20, note that the bottom edge of pattern piece 2 is marked with a dashed line. This edge does not get turned because piece 3 will be placed on top of it on this edge. Simply let the ⅛" seam allowance extend outward. Turn the other edges as usual.

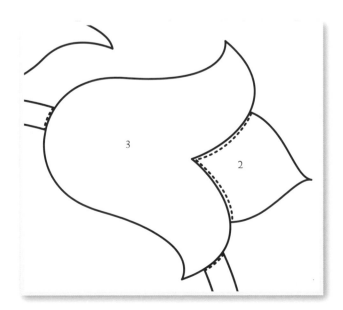

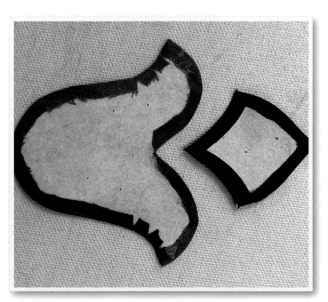

,,, when your appliqué has points: *Begin by applying the glue stick and clipping any inside curves. Before you turn the point, put a small amount of Liquid Stitch on the tip of the point. Heat-set after you finish turning. Put more Liquid Stitch on the point to bond the fibers permanently so your point will not fray. Heat-set the entire piece again. Clip off the excess fabric in the seam allowance of the point.*

Putting the Appliqué Pieces onto the Background

Cut the background fabric 2" larger than the finished size of the block. You will trim it to the size you need after it is finished.

Sharon's Tip: *Press your freezer paper master appliqué pattern onto a piece of cotton batting for a great working surface.*

Fold the background square into quarters, right sides together, and press the folds lightly with an iron. With the wrong side of fabric toward the master pattern, align the center of the background square over the center of the master pattern.

Secure the fabric to the pattern with pins. If you can't see the pattern lines through the fabric, a light box will be helpful.

Starting with appliqué piece 1, put a line of basting glue on the edges. You can use water-soluble glue or my preference, Liquid Stitch.

Place the piece in position on the background and heat-set. Repeat this process with the remaining pieces. Keep in mind that a portion of piece 2 will be overlapped by piece 3.

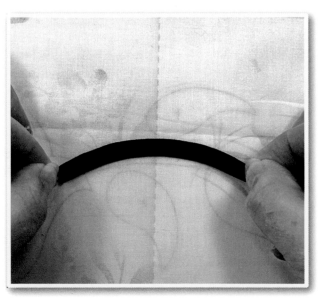

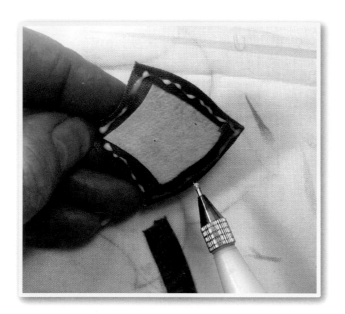

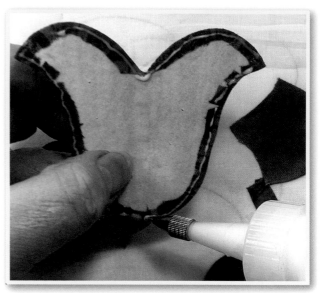

Get Ready to Sew Your Gorgeous Applique Block!

Set up your machine to do a zigzag stitch. You will want to set the stitch length at 1.0 and the stitch width at .9 or 1.1. Use these settings as your starting point, keeping in mind that all machines are different. Adjust your machine's zigzag to get the length and width that works best for you.

Use size 75/11 machine embroidery needles for the best results. Adjust your needle to the center position and decrease your top tension just a little bit.

Use only polyester monofilament thread, threading your machine as you normally would.

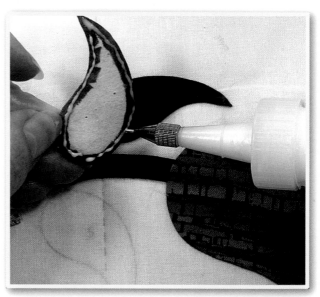

Sharon's Tip: *Put the spool in a cup and your thread will flow more smoothly.*

The tension on the bobbin will need to be tightened, so you can put the thread through the wing of the bobbin, if your bobbin case is equipped with one. If not, you can tighten the screw on the bobbin case one-quarter turn to get the same result.

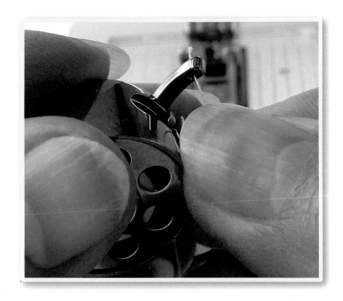

Lock your beginning and ending stitch as you sew. *The left swing of the zigzag stitch should stitch the appliqué piece and the right swing should stitch the background.* When you finish sewing the applique, backstitch several stitches then clip the top thread close to the fabric, leaving a 1" tail on the back. Continue until the entire block has been sewn.

Wash your block with Synthrapol following the mixing instructions on the bottle. Soak the block for at least two hours to remove all the glue. Rinse twice. Let air dry and press flat.

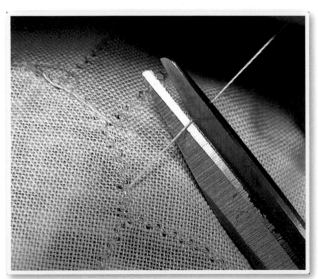

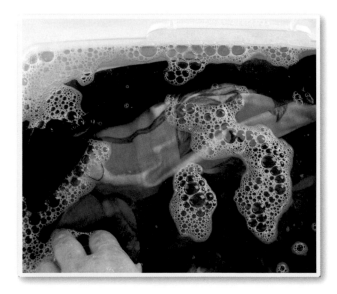

Tulip Wreath Appliqué Pattern

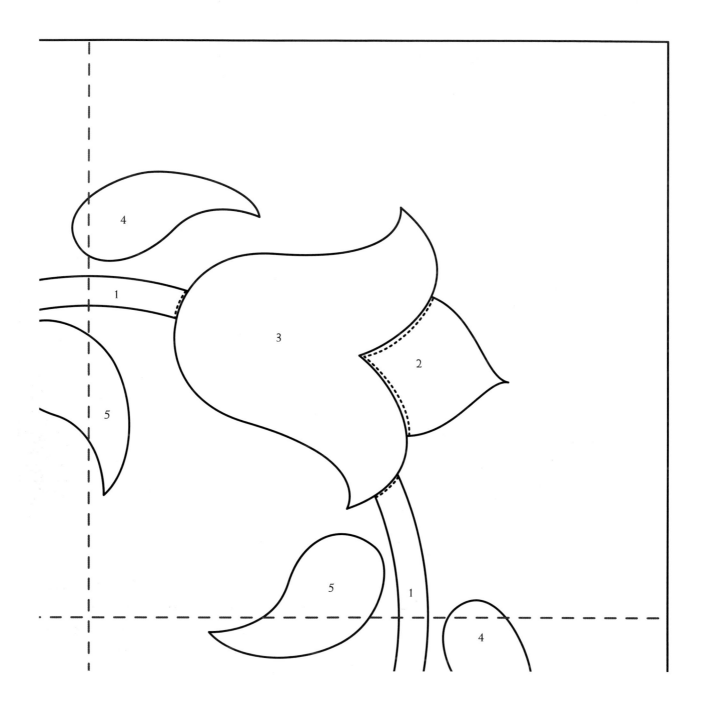

A New Way to
Raw-edge
Appliqué

Before you start to appliqué prewash all of your fabrics as instructed on page 8. Remember not to wash your background fabric.

Sharon's Tip: *The secret to success with my raw-edge appliqué technique is that you MUST spray starch your appliqué fabric at least three or four times. Basically you want to starch it within an inch of its life.*

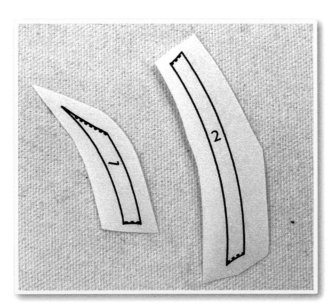

Make five copies of your chosen pattern on the dull side of freezer paper. One copy will be used as a master appliqué foundation pattern and the other four copies are for cutting templates.

Cut the templates apart, leaving extra space outside the lines.

Press the templates on the *right side* of the starched appliqué fabrics. With smooth strokes, cut the pieces on the line, except where you see dashed lines. You will want to add a ¼" allowance to those edges since they will be covered by other pieces.

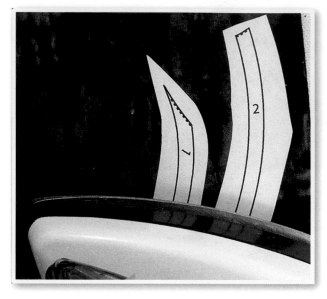

Putting the Appliqué Pieces onto the Background

Cut the block background 2" larger than the finished size of the block. Fold the background square into quarters, right sides together, and lightly press the folds with an iron.

Sharon's Tip: *Press your freezer paper master appliqué pattern onto a piece of cotton batting for a great working surface.*

Align the center of the square over the center of the master pattern. Secure the fabric to the pattern with pins. If you can't see the pattern lines, a light box will be helpful.

Turn piece 1, wrong side up (paper side down). Put a line of Liquid Stitch right on the edge so the piece will be secure on the background. While the glue is still wet, position the piece on the background.

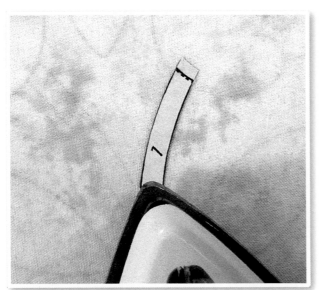

Heat-set the piece and remove the freezer paper while it is still warm. If you have used a basting glue rather than the Liquid Stitch, you may see a shadow of the glue showing through to the front. This will disappear when you wash your block.

Sharon's Tip: *My preference is to use Liquid Stitch instead of a water-soluble basting glue. However, if you feel a little unsure of your placement, use the water-soluble glue since it is easier to reposition. Just be extra careful you don't miss any spots when you are sewing down your appliqué piece.*

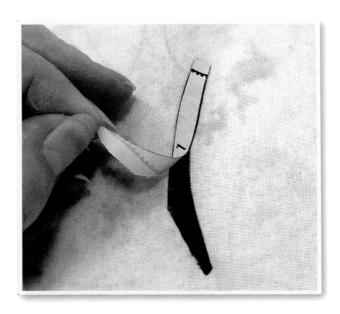

Sharon's Tip for ...

... when your appliqué has sharp and pointy tips:

The sharp points on pieces, such as the leaves, need a bit more care or they will fray. Put a small amount of Liquid Stitch on the wrong side of any points. Then add a thin line of glue around the edge. Put in place and heat-set — remember to remove the freezer paper while it is still warm.

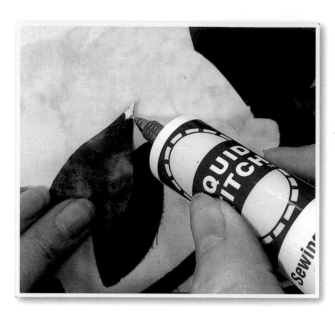

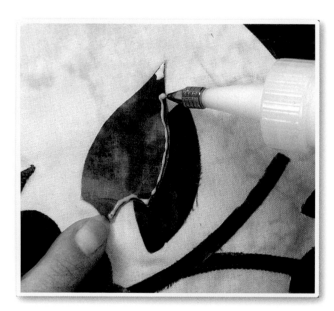

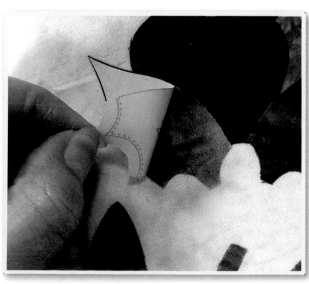

Get Ready to Sew Your Beautiful Block

Set your machine up to stitch a blanket stitch. Put your needle in the down and center position. Adjust your stitch length to 1.8 and the stitch width to 2.0.

I like to use a straight stitch foot as you see in the photo. Be sure to test the space your needle has in your straight stitch foot by slowly turning the sewing machine wheel by hand. If you prefer, you can also use a zigzag foot or open toe embroidery foot with great results.

To make the tension on the bobbin tighter than on the top tension, put the thread through the wing of the bobbin, if your bobbin case is equipped with one. If not, then you can tighten the screw on the bobbin case one-quarter turn to get the same result.

Match your thread to the appliqué color if you want the stitching to blend in. If you prefer a contrasting effect, you can use one color for the whole project.

Use the top thread to pull a long tail of the bobbin thread to the top of your work. This will give you more control and will prevent the creation of knots underneath.

10 Stitch around the appliqué with a blanket stitch. When you are finished, leave a long enough tail on the top thread to pull it through to the back. Tie a knot with the bobbin and top threads.

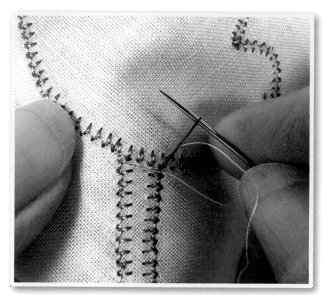

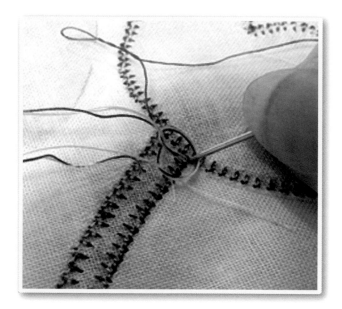

11 Use a needle to bury the thread tails between the background and the appliqué piece so they won't show through when the top is quilted.

Sharon's Tip: *If you don't like the idea of burying all of your thread tails using a needle, simply trim them to measure approximately an inch or smaller, dab a little Liquid Stitch on them and heat-set them to the underside of the appliqué. Pay attention that you are gluing the threads behind the matching appliqué — you don't want to give your beautiful appliqué block varicose veins.*

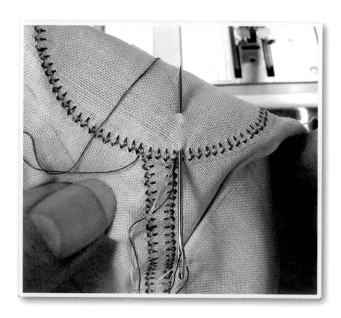

Berry Patch Appliqué Pattern

Inspiration quilt

**Double Daisy
quilt idea ~**
*By simply turning
the block in different
directions you can
make this beautiful
design.*

For a 12" finished block, enlarge pattern 200%

Inspiration quilt

Purple Daisy quilt idea ~

Pick two contrasting colors for your backgrounds and let the pieced sashing do all of the heavy lifting – design wise.

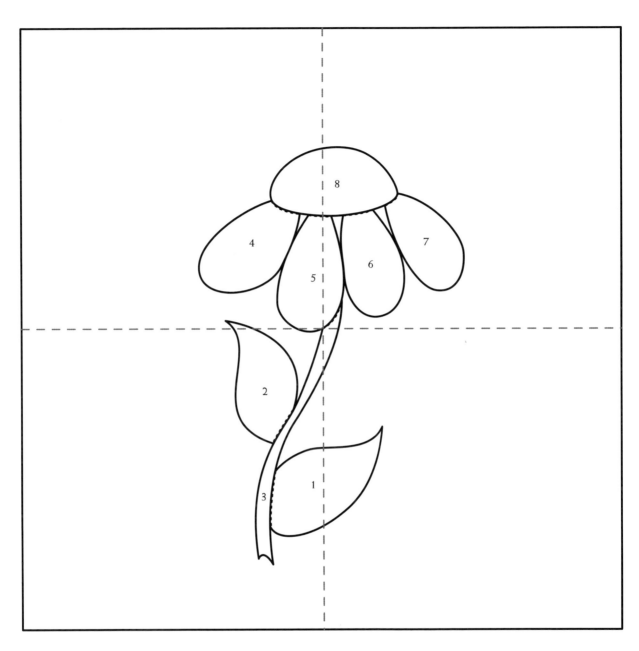

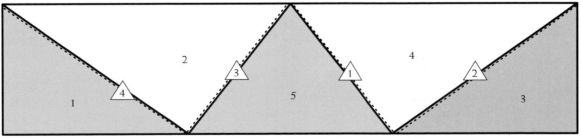

For a 12" finished block, enlarge pattern 200%

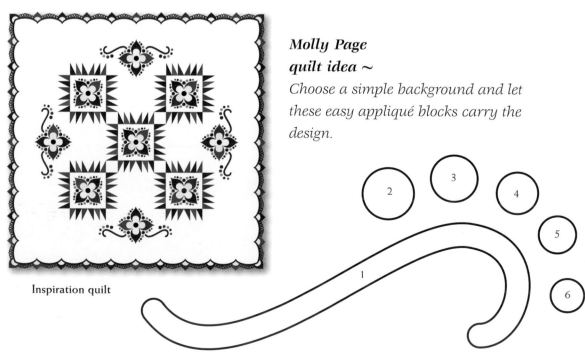

Inspiration quilt

Molly Page
quilt idea ~

Choose a simple background and let these easy appliqué blocks carry the design.

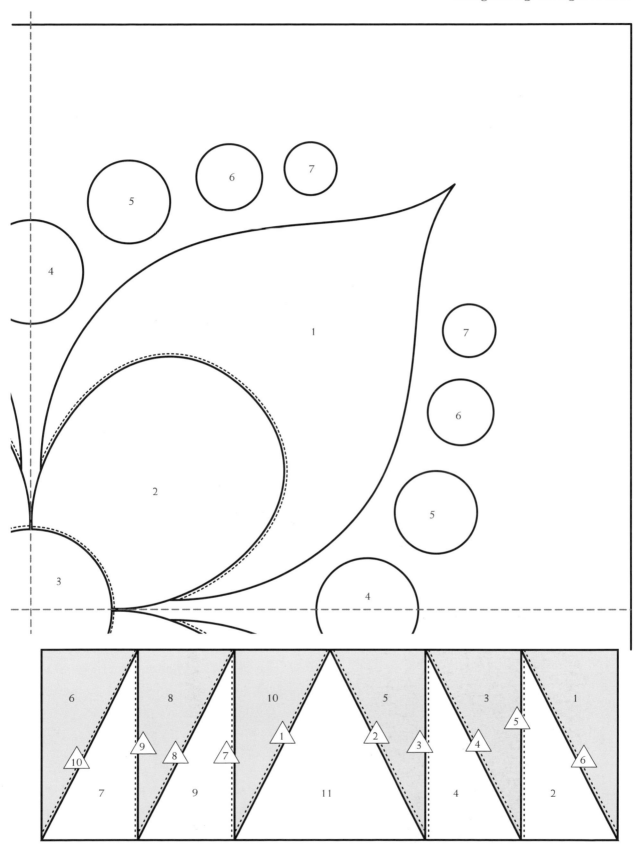

For a 12" finished block, enlarge pattern 200%

Paperless *Paper* Piecing

Paperless paper piecing is a fabulously easy technique that lets you "paper piece" designs with the precision that traditional paper piecing is known for while giving you many freedoms you don't have when using the traditional paper foundations. Plus there are no pesky foundation papers to pull out. With this technique, freezer paper is used for the master foundation pattern as well as for the individual templates. Don't let the T-word scare you ... it really is easy.

Preparing for Paperless Paper Piecing

This technique works very well on precise angular designs such as the Compass block in SCARLET SERENADE. Let us start by gathering the needed supplies. You will find the pattern for the Compass block on page 73.

Make two copies of the pattern on the dull side of the freezer paper. One copy will be used as a master foundation pattern. Cut out this pattern leaving a margin of paper around the outer edge and set aside.

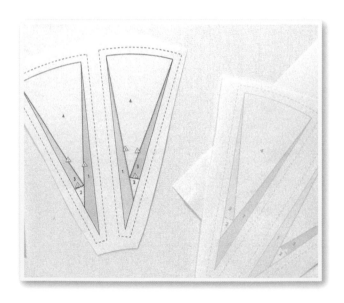

The other copy will be cut apart to serve as individual templates. Place this copy of your pattern on another piece of freezer paper, both shiny sides down. Using an iron, press the pieces firmly together to create a permanent bond. This will give your templates more stability.

Begin by cutting out the entire pattern leaving a margin of paper around the outer edge. Then cut into separate pieces by cutting on the solid lines. These are your templates.

Press template sections onto the wrong side of the fabric. Cut the fabric around the template section, leaving about a ½" seam allowance.

The edge indicated by the **small** dotted line is the one you will need to turn. Using a stencil brush, paint some starch on this seam allowance.

While the starch is still wet, fold the seam allowance over the template and press until dry. Pull the template off the fabric piece and press again if necessary.

Repeat this process for pieces 2 and 3.

Putting the Pieces Together

Press the master foundation pattern to your pressing surface, shiny side down. Pin piece 1 into position, **wrong side up**. It is important to make sure the fold aligns with the seam line on the master pattern.

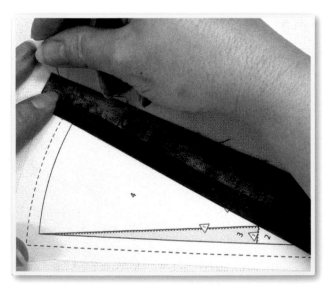

Place a thin line of basting glue on the fold line of piece 1. Make sure you place the glue ONLY along the edge where piece 2 will overlap it.

Place piece 2, wrong side up, on the master foundation pattern. Pay attention that the fold of piece 2 aligns with the seam line on the master pattern. Heat-set.

On piece 2, put a fine line of basting glue on the fold where piece 3 will go. Place piece 3; heat-set.

Place a fine line of glue on the fold of pieces 1, 2, and 3. Be sure you are placing the glue ONLY where piece 4 will overlap them. Place piece 4 into position and heat-set.

Sharon's Tip: *Because you are paper piecing without paper, you can press the seam allowances in any direction. I like to press them toward the darker color, which helps when quilting. Then I can quilt the background without crossing a bulky area, and the seam allowances do not shadow through to the front of the quilt.*

Sewing the Pieces Together

The numbers in the triangles on the master pattern indicate the sewing sequence. As you see, they represent a logical sewing order that you can apply to any block you make using this technique.

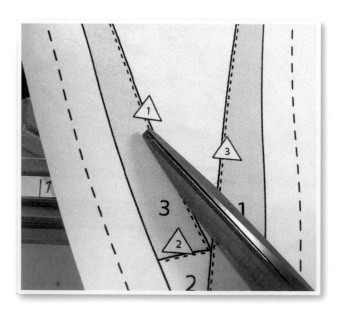

Set up your machine with a 1.8 stitch length (about 14 stitches to the inch). Use a quarter-inch quilting or an open toe embroidery foot, whichever is more comfortable for you. Put your needle in the center and down position.

Lift the fabric unit off of the master pattern. Open seam 1 (it will be marked on your master foundation pattern with a small triangle) until you can see the fold. Sew directly on the fold.

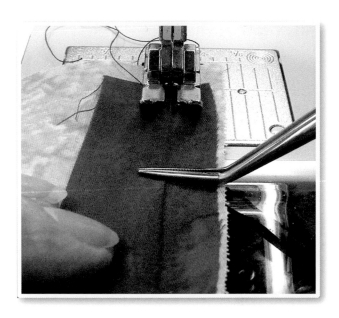

Trim the seam allowance to ¼". Following the numerical sequence, sew the rest of the seams in this manner.

Press the master pattern onto the right side of the pieced unit. Make sure to align the pattern lines with the seam lines. Trim the completed unit so the seam allowance measures ¼". Make as many units as your pattern requires.

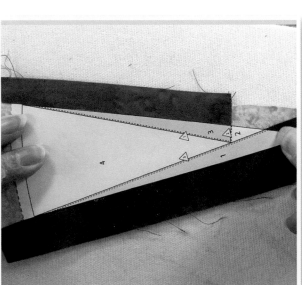

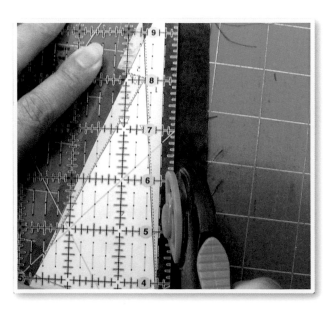

Sawtooth Borders

Have you ever pieced a border and when you were finally finished, found it didn't fit? I think all of us have had that frustrating experience at one time or another. But don't give up on pieced borders just yet. Paperless paper piecing can be very helpful in getting pieced borders to come out just the right size. I chose to make the sawtooth borders for SCARLET SERENADE using the following technique:

On page 74 you will find the patterns for the sawtooth border. Prepare border templates by making 2 copies of them on the dull side of freezer paper. You will need one copy to use as a master foundation pattern and copy number two will be cut apart to serve as individual templates.

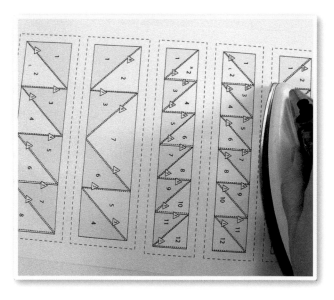

Sharon's Tip: *On average, templates can be used 7 to 10 times before the edges get soft and no longer give you a crisp fold. Make yourself enough templates to start a little assembly line when it comes to gluing and sewing your border pieces together and you'll be finished in no time.*

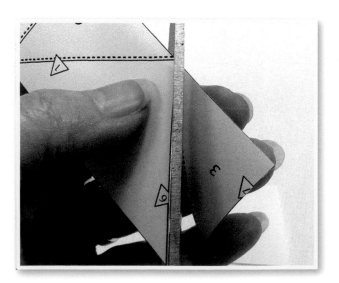

To start, make 2 copies of the sawtooth border pattern on the dull side of the freezer paper. One copy will be used as a master foundation pattern. Cut out this pattern, leaving extra paper outside of the outer solid line (which is the seam line) and set aside.

The other copy of the border pattern will be cut apart to serve as individual templates. Place this copy of your pattern on another piece of freezer paper, both shiny sides down. Using an iron, press the pieces firmly together to create a permanent bond. This will give your templates more stability. Begin by cutting out the pattern on the outer solid line. Then cut into separate pieces by cutting on the remaining solid lines. These are your templates.

Sharon's Tip: *I have shaded the sawtooth triangles so it is easier for you to tell them apart from the background.*

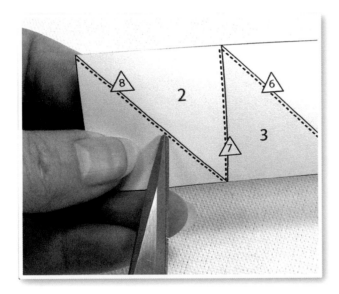

Press all of the templates you are working with onto the wrong side of the fabrics you are using. Cut the fabric around the template section leaving a seam allowance of approximately ½".

Using a stencil brush, paint some starch on the seam allowance indicated with a small dashed line. While the starch is still wet, fold the seam allowance over the template and press until dry. (Notice that piece 7 does not have any dashed lines.) Peel templates off.

Press the master pattern to your pressing surface. Pin the first triangle into position, **wrong side up**. It is important to make sure the diagonal fold is aligned with the seam line on the master pattern.

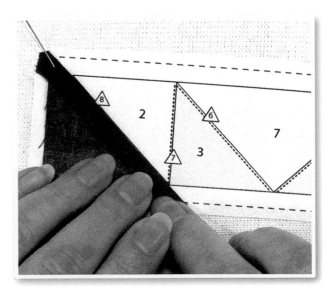

Place a line of basting glue on the fold of the first triangle (diagonal seam). Place second triangle into position, this time making sure to align the vertical folded edge of that triangle on the seam line.

Repeat these steps following the indicated numerical sequence.

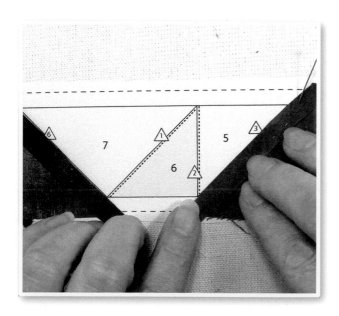

Set up your machine with a 1.8 stitch length (about 14 stitches to the inch). Use a quarter-inch open toe foot. Put your needle in the center and in the down position.

Lift the glued sawtooth unit off of the master pattern. Open seam 1 until you can see the fold. Sew directly on the fold.

Trim the seam allowance to measure ¼". Continue to sew the seams in numerical order, trimming them down to ¼" as you work.

When you are ready to trim all of your border units, start by cutting excess paper off of the master foundation pattern by cutting on the solid line around the outer edge. Press the master pattern onto the right side of the sawtooth border unit. Make sure to align the pattern lines with the seam lines. Trim the unit so outer seam allowance measures ¼".

Sew sawtooth units together to make the desired length of border.

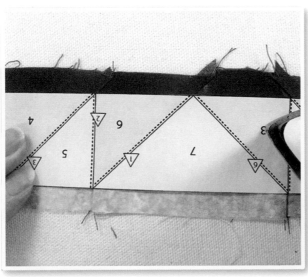

Approximate quilt size 102" x 102"

Making
Scarlet
Serenade

...One-on-One with Sharon

Yellow background	7¼ yards
Red corner triangles	2¼ yards
8 Yellows	¼ each
9 Reds	¼ each
7 Greens	¼ each
Backing	9⅝ yards
Binding	1 yard

Be sure to cut out border pieces before you cut out your blocks

Yellow border	4 borders 11½" wide, cut on the lengthwise grain 105" long
Yellow blocks	9 squares 20" x 20" You will later trim them to measure 17¼" x 17¼".
Red corners	2 squares 37⅞" x 37⅞", cut in half diagonally once
Binding	11 strips 2¼" wide

Scarlet Serenade ~ 2005

Originally I designed and pieced this quilt in 2000 and then "aged" the top until 2005, which is when I finally quilted it. It has won the Best of Show Award in Houston, Texas, in 2005 and then went on to win the Best Longarm Quilting Award at the AQS Show in Paducah, Kentucky.

Appliqué Blocks

Make the 5 unique SCARLET SERENADE blocks and 4 border sections. Patterns are found on pages 60–71. If you need to refresh yourself on the basics of turned-edge appliqué technique, refer to pages 11–19.

Use the following advanced turned-edge appliqué techniques where necessary

Making Perfect Circles

Apply glue stick to circle foundation and heat-set to wrong side of fabric. Trim fabric around circle foundation leaving an ⅛" turn-under allowance. Apply glue stick to the allowance and the edges of the template. Using two cuticle sticks to make small tucks as you go around the edge of the circle, turn the seam allowance over the foundation. If your circle starts looking angular, you are making your tucks too big.

Hold the circle with your cuticle stick as you gently press the edge back. Turn it right side up and press your perfect circle from the top.

Getting Crisp Tips on Your Crescent Shapes

The secret to making perfect crescent shapes is to work on each side of the crescent separately. Begin by putting glue stick only on the inside curve and clip, stopping a few threads short of the foundation.

Next, put a small amount of Liquid Stitch at the tips. Using a pinching action, gently turn the inside edge against the foundation. Heat-set.

Now put glue stick on the outward curve and add Liquid Stitch to the tips again.

Using the slanted end of your cuticle stick, turn in the excess fabric on the tips. Then using a pinching action, gently turn the outward curve against the foundation. Heat-set.

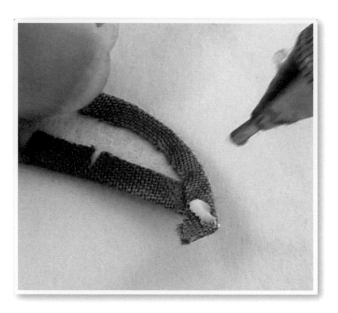

Put a small amount of Liquid Stitch on the tips and turn excess fabric of the point back. Heat-set the tips.

Trim excess fabric that hangs over the finished edge.

Apply a little more Liquid Stitch on the tips. Let it dry before applying it to the background.

Repeat these steps with all remaining crescent shapes.

Making Applique Units

Many times you can combine appliqué pieces into a unit before applying it to the background.

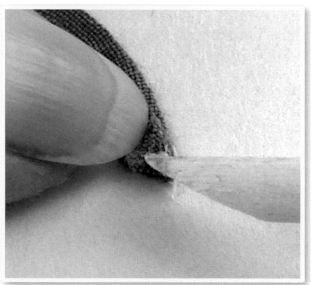

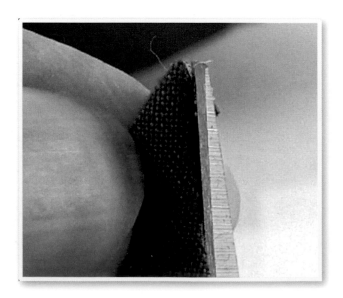

Start by preparing the individual appliqués you will need for that section. Place appliqué pieces wrong side up on your master appliqué pattern.

The secret is that you will glue them together in exactly the reverse order of how you would place them on the background if you were not making a unit first.

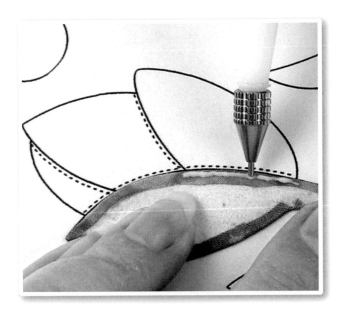

In other words, the piece that would normally go on last will be the one you place on the foundation first. Add a line of water soluble glue only along the edge of the appliqué that will be covered by the next piece.

Lay the next appliqué piece in position and heat-set. Keep working in this manner until the section is complete. Be sure to heat-set after each piece.

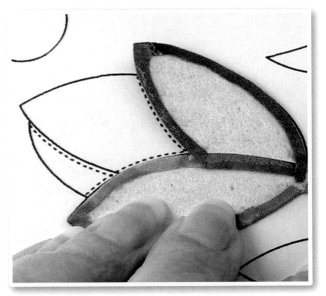

Once your appliqué unit is finished, put a line of water-soluble glue along the outside edge of the entire unit and place it on the background where it belongs.

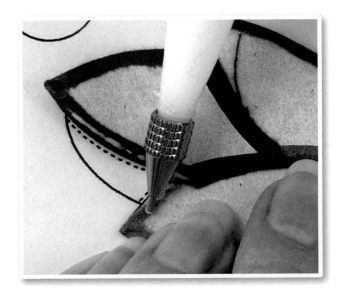

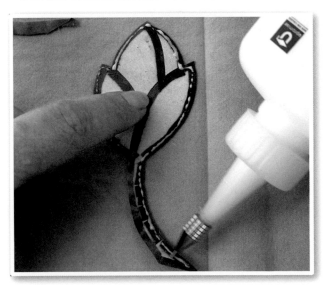

Compass Blocks

To make the Compass blocks you will need to follow the instructions for Paperless Paper Piecing illustrated on pages 34–39. Use the remaining yellow 20" squares and an assortment of reds for your compass points.

Refer to page 73 for the Compass template pattern. Note that sections A and B are mirror images of one another.

Make two copies of each section on freezer paper. You will use one copy for making the templates and the other copy as your master foundation pattern.

Making the Compass

Following the instructions on pages 34–39, make 32 of section A and 32 of section B.

Sew section A and B together. Make 32.

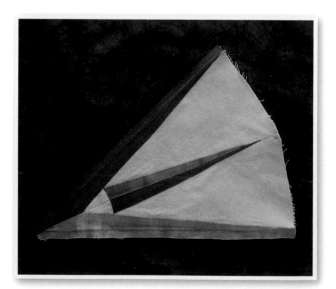

Sew A/B units together to make quarter circles. Then sew quarter circles together again to make half circles. Sew half circles together to form the compass as illustrated. Make four.

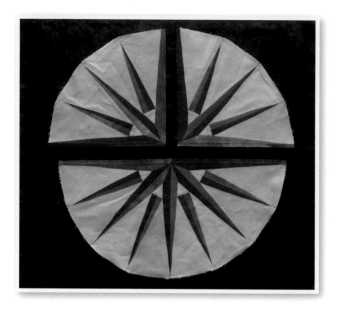

Measure the distance across the points of the compass. Be sure to measure from point to point NOT including the seam allowance.

Sharon's Tip: *Use grosgrain ribbon for both measuring and drawing your circles. Mark the distance between the compass tip and center on the ribbon. Push a pin through ribbon and freezer paper on one of the pencil marks. Push the tip of a pencil through the other mark on the ribbon. You can now draw a perfect circle, or partial circle. Always measure the sewn compass rather than the master template.*

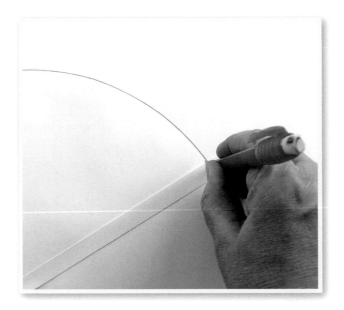

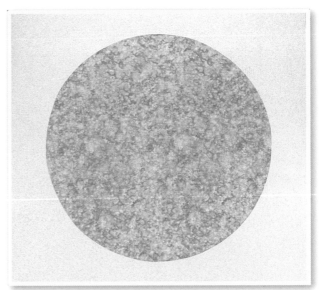

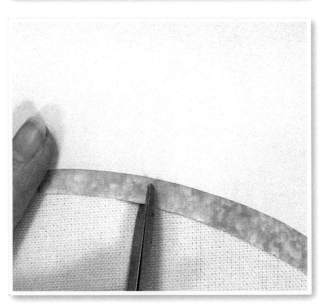

Press two sheets of freezer paper together and cut into a 20" square. Draw a circle the same size as the point to point measurcment of the compass onto the freezer paper. Be sure to center the circle within the square. Cut out the circle making sure to keep the frame intact.

Press this freezer-paper template onto a 20" square of yellow fabric. Cut out the fabric center leaving about a ½" seam allowance. Clip the seam allowance every ½".

Spray a little spray starch into the can's lid. Using a stencil brush, paint some starch on the seam allowance and then turn it back against the edge of the template. Press until dry. Peel the template off while still warm.

Fold the fabric frame into quarters and mark the creases by lightly pressing them with an iron.

Place the frame on top of the compass, both right side up, matching the pressed lines to the compass points. Pin together at the fold lines.

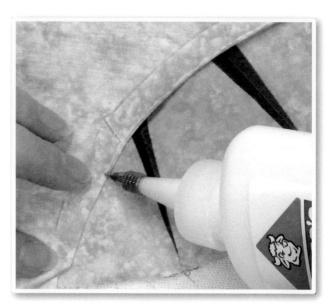

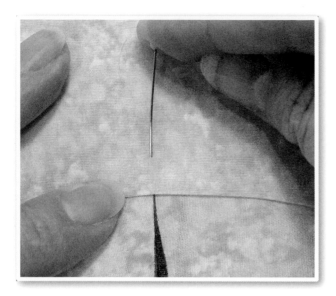

Fold back a quarter of the frame without removing the pins until you can see the seam allowance. Put a thin line of glue on the edge of the fold. Gently pat compass and frame section into place. Heat-set. Repeat this gluing process, a quarter at a time all around the compass.

Remove the pins. Unfold the frame enough so you can see the fold line. Sew around the circle on this fold. Trim seam allowance to measure ¼" and press the block flat. Make four compass blocks.

Trim appliqué and compass blocks to measure 17¼" x 17¼". Make sure to keep the appliqué and compass centered within your block.

Putting the Blocks Together

Sew blocks together into rows, alternating appliqué and Compass blocks as illustrated in the figure below. Press seams towards applique blocks. Then sew rows together and press the quilt.

Sew sections A and B together into pairs, then sew pairs together into quarter circles. Sew two quarter circle units together for each corner.

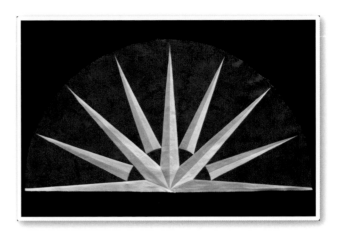

Measure the half compass unit from point to point not including the seam allowance if you are using a ruler. If you prefer to measure using the grosgrain ribbon, be sure to measure from tip to center.

Corners

Enlarge Compass template pattern sections A and B by 225%. Patterns are on page 73. Following the Paperless Paper Piecing technique as before, make 16 sections A and 16 sections B.

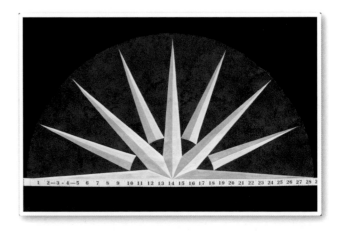

Draw a half circle the same size as the point to point measurement of the compass on a piece of freezer paper. Press onto another piece of freezer paper for extra stability and cut out circle. Find the center of the half-compass frame by lightly creasing the freezer-paper template in half. Mark center of circle with a pencil.

Align center crease of triangle with center mark on your freezer-paper frame template. Be sure to allow for the ¼" seam allowance.

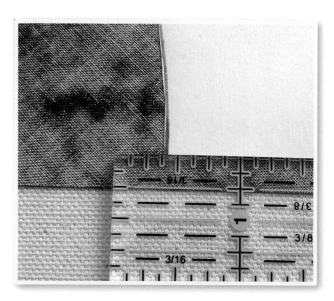

Fold large red coner triangles in half and lightly press to mark center point.

Cut out the fabric center leaving about a ½" seam allowance. Clip, starch, and press seam allowance to the back, against the edge of the template as you did before. Press until dry. Carefully peel template off of the fabric taking care not to stretch the bias edge of the triangle.

Place triangle frame over compass half, both right sides up, matching the pressed line to the center compass point. Pin together.

Fold back half of the frame so you can see the seam allowance and put a thin line of glue on the edge of the fold. Gently pat compass section and frame into place. Heat-set. Repeat on the other side.

Remove the pins. Unfold the frame enough so you can see the fold line. Sew around the half circle on this fold. Trim seam allowance to ¼" and press the corner triangle flat.

Sawtooth Borders

You will need to make three sets of sawtooth borders for this quilt — one small sawtooth border and two large sawtooth borders. Refer to pages 40–43 to familiarize yourself with the Paperless Paper Piecing technique before starting on the sawtooth borders.

It is better to make the border units in one continuous length as illustrated in figure 1, page 56. Make your borders so they have as many teeth as illlustrated. Note that the border side units are shorter than the top/bottom units by one half square triangle on each end.

Make several copies of sawtooth border patterns A, B and C. You will need one set as your master foundation patterns and the additional copies to make your templates. Patterns are on page 74.

Sew the shorter borders to the side of the quilt and the larger borders on the top and bottom as illllustrated.

Figure 1
Small Sawtooth INSIDE Border
Side: make 2

Top/bottom: make 2

Add the compass corner units to your quilt.

To make the remaining sawtooth borders, you will need to use sawtooth border patterns D, E and F. Follow the steps as before using these patterns for your master foundation pattern and templates. Refer to figure 2 for the number of teeth each border needs to have.

Sew inside sawtooth border onto quilt as before.

With raw edges even and right sides together, match the center of the appliquéd border strip to the center of the quilt and pin border and quilt together. Start and stop seam ¼" from the outer edge Be sure to lock your beginning and ending stitches.

Figure 2
Large Sawtooth INSIDE Border
Top/bottom: make 2
Sides: make 2

Large Sawtooth OUTER Border
Top/bottom: make 2
Sides: make 2

Sew border on remaining three sides of quilt starting and stopping ¼" from outer edge. Lay corner flat with ends of border extending outward. Fold top border strip at a 45° angle and press. Put a line of basting glue on the inside edge of the diagonal fold. Heat-set. Unfold corner and sew directly in the crease. Trim seam allowance to measure ¼" and press. Miter remaining three corners following these steps.

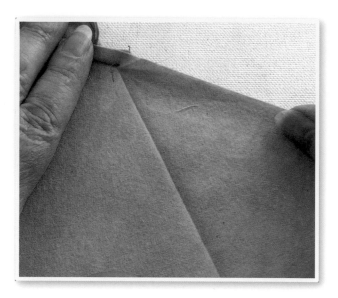

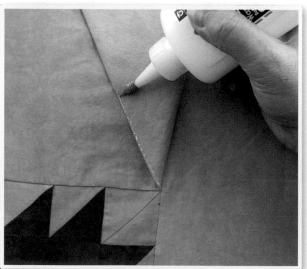

Make a set of master foundation patterns and templates by reducing the compass pattern found on page 73 to 85%. Make four sections A and B. Sew them together to make four quarter units.

Measure quarter compass unit from point tip to center, not including the seam allowance. Draw a quarter circle that size onto freezer-paper frame.

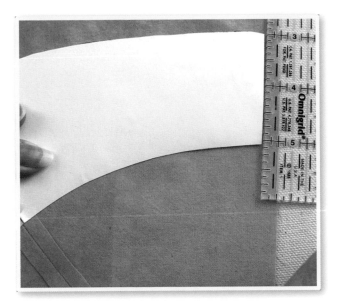

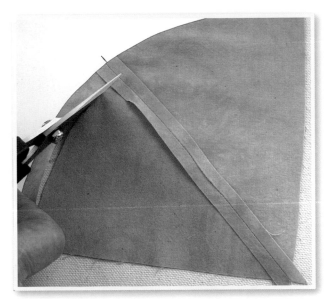

Press frame template onto wrong side of mitered corners. Be sure to allow for your ¼" seam allowance. Cut out quarter circles from the quilt corners leaving ½" seam allowance. Following the same steps as before, inset the quarter compass into the border corners.

Add the outer sawtooth border to your quilt. Press your border to make sure it is lying flat. Quilt as desired and then bind.

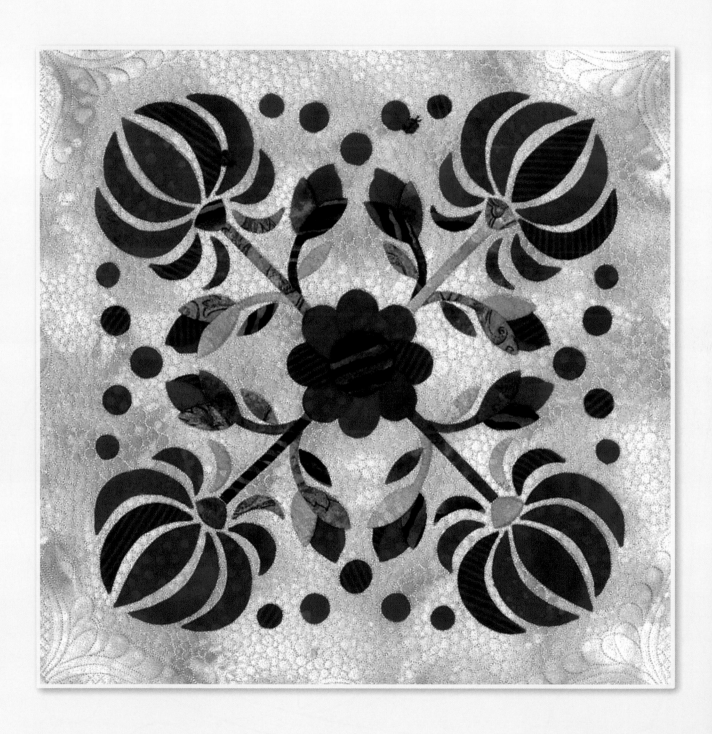

enlarge 200%

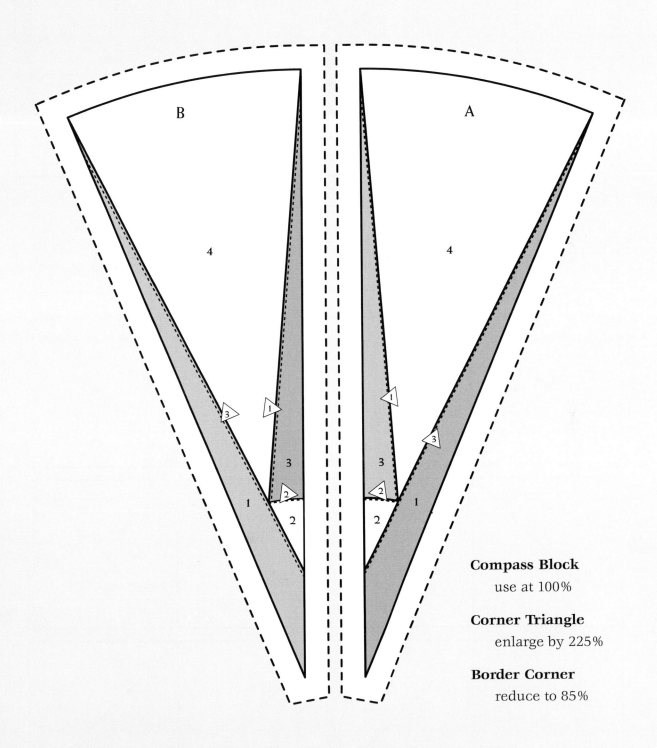

Compass Block
use at 100%

Corner Triangle
enlarge by 225%

Border Corner
reduce to 85%

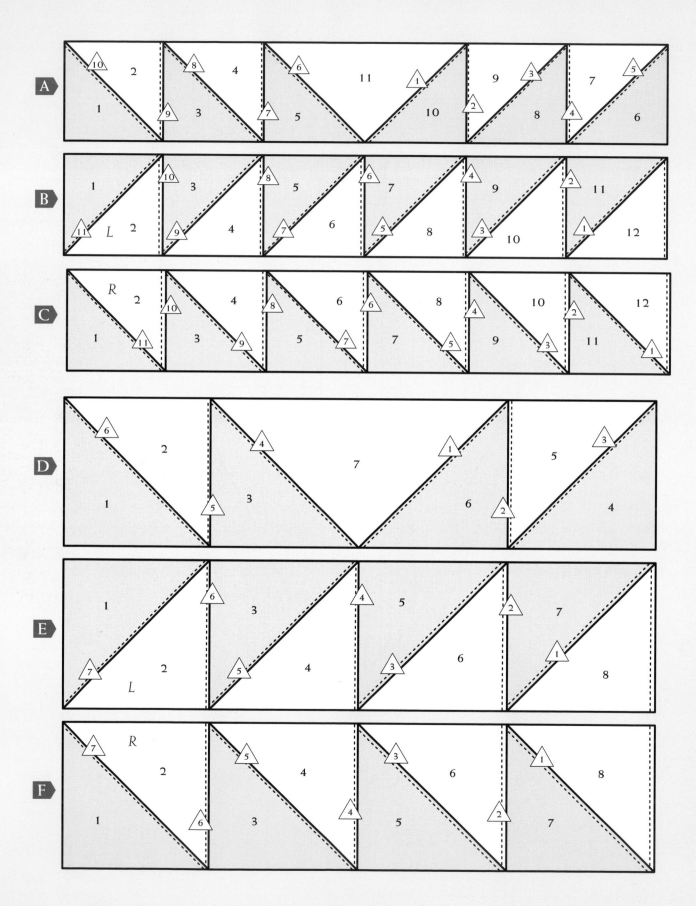

Show
&
Tell

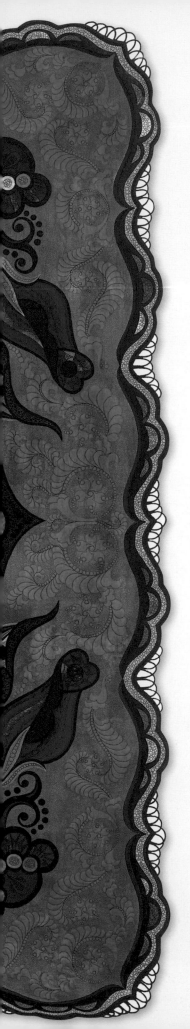

" . . . this is only the beginning. I hope to continue to inspire you through both my teaching and my new creations. You will see many new things from me in the future. I can hardly wait to share what is around the corner."

Sedona Rose ~ *2006*

This visually exciting quilt has the honor of being part of the permanent collection at the American Quilter's Museum in Paducah, Kentucky. On its debut showing in 2006, it won the coveted Best of Show Award at the AQS Quilt Show. Not only is it striking on the front, the back simply glistens with over 100,000 Swarovski® crystals.

Flower of Life ~ 2007

I chose the purple and gold color theme for this quilt mainly because these colors are so happy in each other's company and at the same time they also contrast very well. This was an important consideration since there are many small details within the appliqué and much intricate quilting that needed to show. To get just the right shades of purple and gold, I hand dyed these fabrics myself.

Spin Dancer ~ 2007

This is the second quilt I made using all of my own hand-dyed fabrics. My intent was to find a fresh new color combination for this quilt. I also wanted to showcase my corded binding technique. As a special touch, I added embroidered epaulets in the binding. Many quilters tend to overlook the design potential borders and bindings offer.

Prim & Proper ~ 2005

This is another example of how machine appliqué can take on the look of exquisite handwork. Originally I designed this quilt as a class sample and later made it into a commercial pattern. Just wait until you see what I'm doing with it now!

Molly Page (Royal Dance) ~ 2007

This quilt was designed by my daughter, Cristy Fincher. It started life as ROYAL DANCE but we have rechristened it to MOLLY PAGE in honor of our new grandaughter. Molly was born on January 9, 2007, with severe heart defects. After one open-heart surgery she is doing well, although she will have to undergo several more surgeries later.

I made this quilt using my appliqué and piec-liqué techniques. I love Cristy's overall design, particularly the scalloped border.

Hearts & Apron Strings ~ *2002*

This quilt commemorates my daughter's wedding day. I think all mothers can relate to the feelings of joy, pride, and even a little sadness this day can bring. While making this quilt, I took many walks down memory lane. They really do grow up too fast. You may have already guessed that at heart, Cristy is a traditionalist.

Victorian Flame ~ *1999*

This quilt won the Best of Show Award in 1999 at the Jinny Beyer Borders on Brilliance contest held in Houston, Texas. I made this quilt entirely by hand using Jinny Beyer border prints. I like to encourage my students to think beyond the everyday limits when it comes to using fabrics. This is a good example of using strong vertical prints in new and interesting ways.

Wind River Majesty ~ *2000*

This quilt showing the leaping elk was named after the breathtaking mountains in Wyoming, my husband's home state. In Indian folklore it is said that the elk came to earth because he had many things to teach us. His power comes from endurance. While other animals have much more speed, none can equal his stamina and so he often outruns even the fastest mountain cats.

High Country King ~ *2000*

I used to wonder if two Leos could happily live together. If you've wondered about that too, the answer is a resounding YES. I made this machine pieced and appliquéd quilt of this regal lion for my husband and gave it to him on his birthday.

→ Piece *by* Piece **Machine Appliqué** ← *Sharon Schamber & Cristy Fincher*

Lily ~ *2002*

It is good to remember that in quilting, the sky is literally the limit. This small quilt was made for a painting class that I taught for several years. Notice how you can give the floral appliqué real depth by simply painting and shading the fabric.

Windblown Acanthus ~ 2004

This is one of my original quilts that was inspired by a Jacobean design. I wanted to give it a new look by using strong and distinct contrasts. For some extra glitz, I added Swarovski crystals.

One Rose ~ 2006

Beautiful appliqué doesn't have to be complicated. This small wallhanging is a great example of how wonderful simple raw-edge appliqué can look. I originally made it as a sample for a longarm class that I currently teach.

Meet *the* Authors

Sharon Schamber

I started sewing when I was six years old; that is when my Aunt Joe taught me how to sew. At the ripe old age of 12, I started buying clothes from Goodwill so I could take them apart and then sew them together again. For many years since, I used my creative energies in a successful career designing and making bridal and pageant wear.

When I retired from the bridal business, somehow the quilting bug bit me. In many ways I starting quilting much like most other quilters. The thousands of questions of what was "right" and what was "wrong" literally made my head spin. Not to mention the lingo. I found that I had to achieve a scant quarter but I needed to buy a fat quarter. Translating all those quilting terms was almost like learning a different language.

While the learning curve for a novice quilter is fairly steep, I was learning to quilt on my own in the middle of the Arizona desert. My teachers were quilting books, my imagination, and all of the childhood memories I could scrounge up of my grandmother quilting in the '60s. Thankfully, I discovered that we do many things differently today.

Even from the very beginning, I have always loved appliqué best. The results that can be achieved are so beautiful it almost broke my heart when I discovered that this technique was impossible for me to do using traditional methods. You see, I have inherited a tremor from both of my parents.

To my joy, I have been able to develop many techniques that give you a beautiful hand-done result using a sewing machine. Just wait and until you see how much fun it is making beautiful appliqué blocks using my easy techniques. But I promise you this is only the beginning. I hope to continue to inspire you through both my teaching and my new creations. You will see many different things from me in the future. I can hardly wait to share what is around the corner.

Cristy Fincher

I grew up watching my mom sew. It was deliriously fun to watch those beautiful fabrics turn into "princess dresses" from my special perch atop her sewing table. It would be easy to say that all that early fabric exposure has led to my lifelong love and admiration for sewing and design, but one does have to wonder if some of it isn't genetic.

As an adult it was easy for me to fall in love with quilting. I began piecing by hand but my impatience of wanting to see the design come together soon led me to use the machine for piecing and appliqué.

As an elementary school teacher, I enjoy teaching my students about quilting and helping them put together blocks for special projects. But I haven't been able to stop there — I truly enjoy teaching adults as well. It's pure satisfaction to see quilters' faces light up as they learn new techniques.

Other AQS Books

This is only a small selection of the books available from the American Quilter's Society. AQS books are known worldwide for timely topics, clear writing, beautiful color photos, and accurate illustrations and patterns. The following books are available from your local bookseller, quilt shop, or public library.

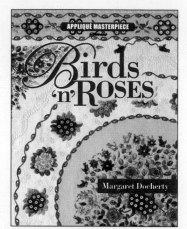

#7013   us$24.95

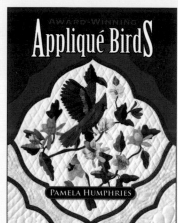

#7494   us$21.95

#5338   us$21.95

#6905   us$24.95

#6681   us$24.95

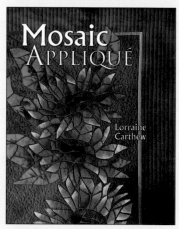

#7071   us$22.95

#6906   us$24.95

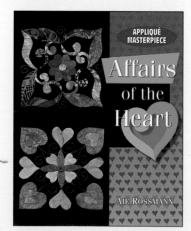

#6517   us$21.95

#7016   us$22.95

Look for these books nationally.
Call or **Visit** our Web site at

1-800-626-5420
www.AmericanQuilter.com